Wichita Mountains Wildlife Refuge Oklahoma

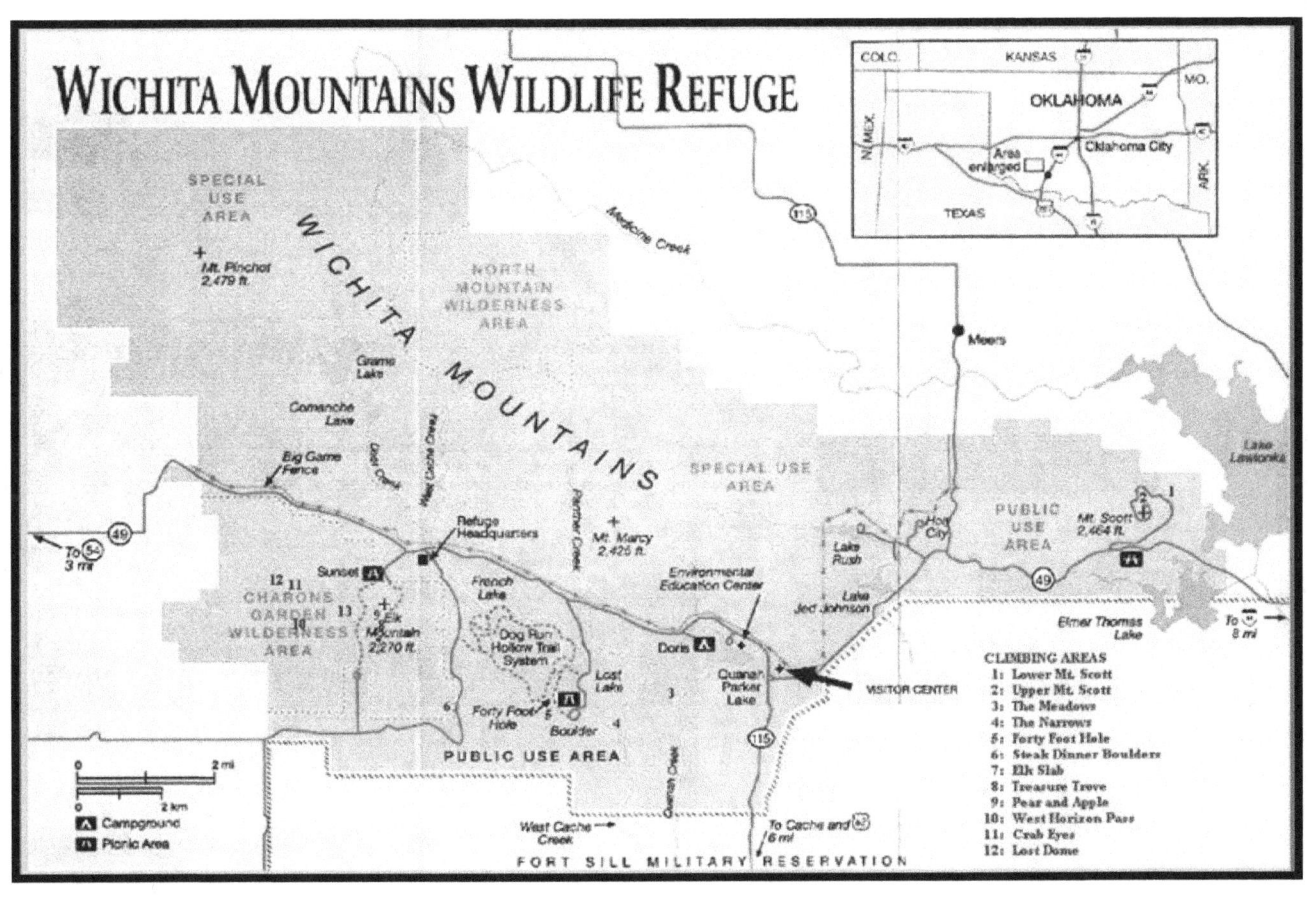

Alle Alexander

Dedicated to:

My nephew and niece, Alex and Ella.
I'm so happy you enjoyed your visit to the Wildlife Refuge. Now because of you two, everyone will get to take home some more memories!

For more information about the Wichita Wildlife Refuge:

Wichita Mountains Wildlife Refuge
 32 Refuge Headquarters
Indiahoma, Oklahoma 73552
580/429-3222 580/429-9323 Fax
https://www.fws.gov/refuge/wichita_mountains/

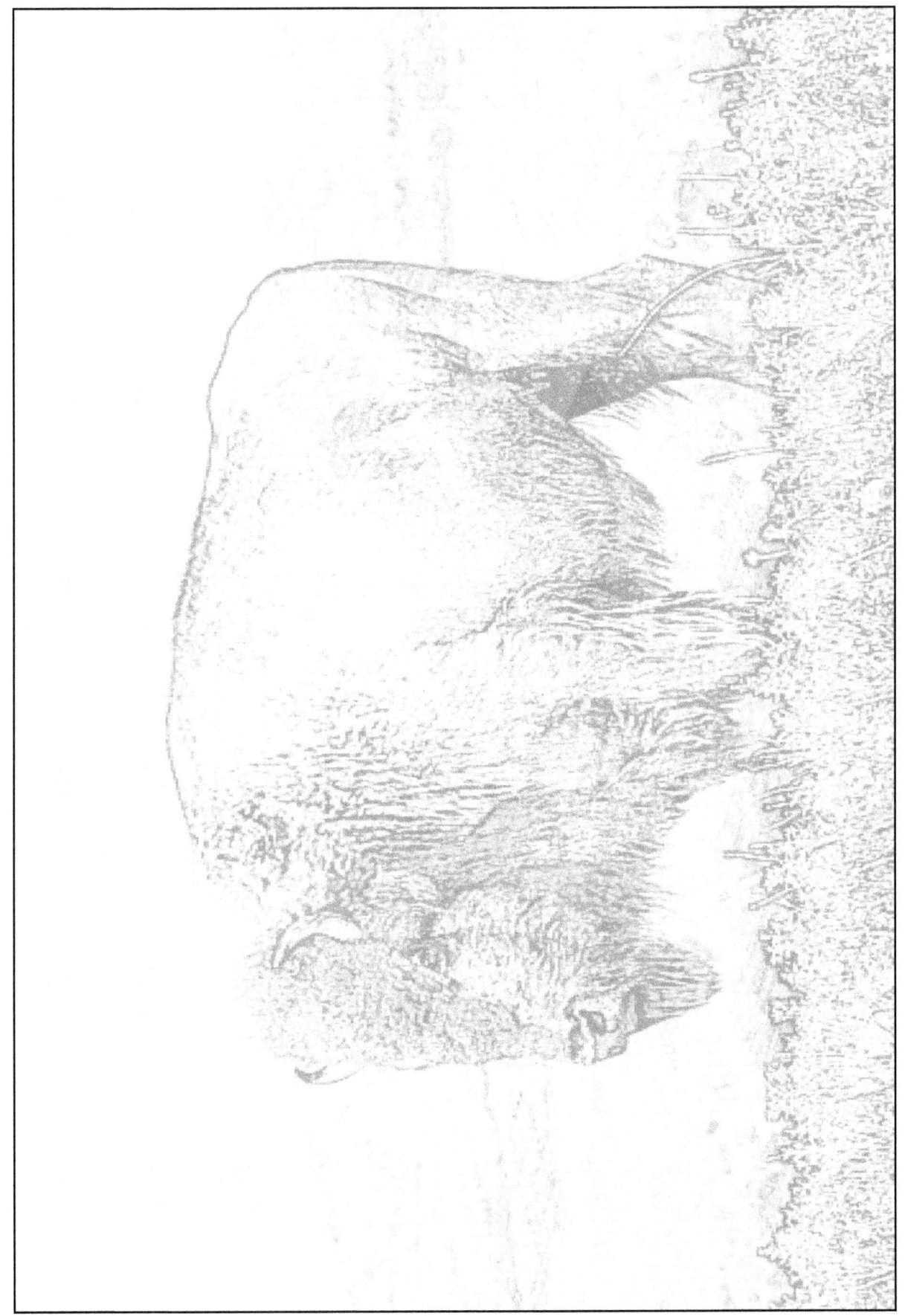

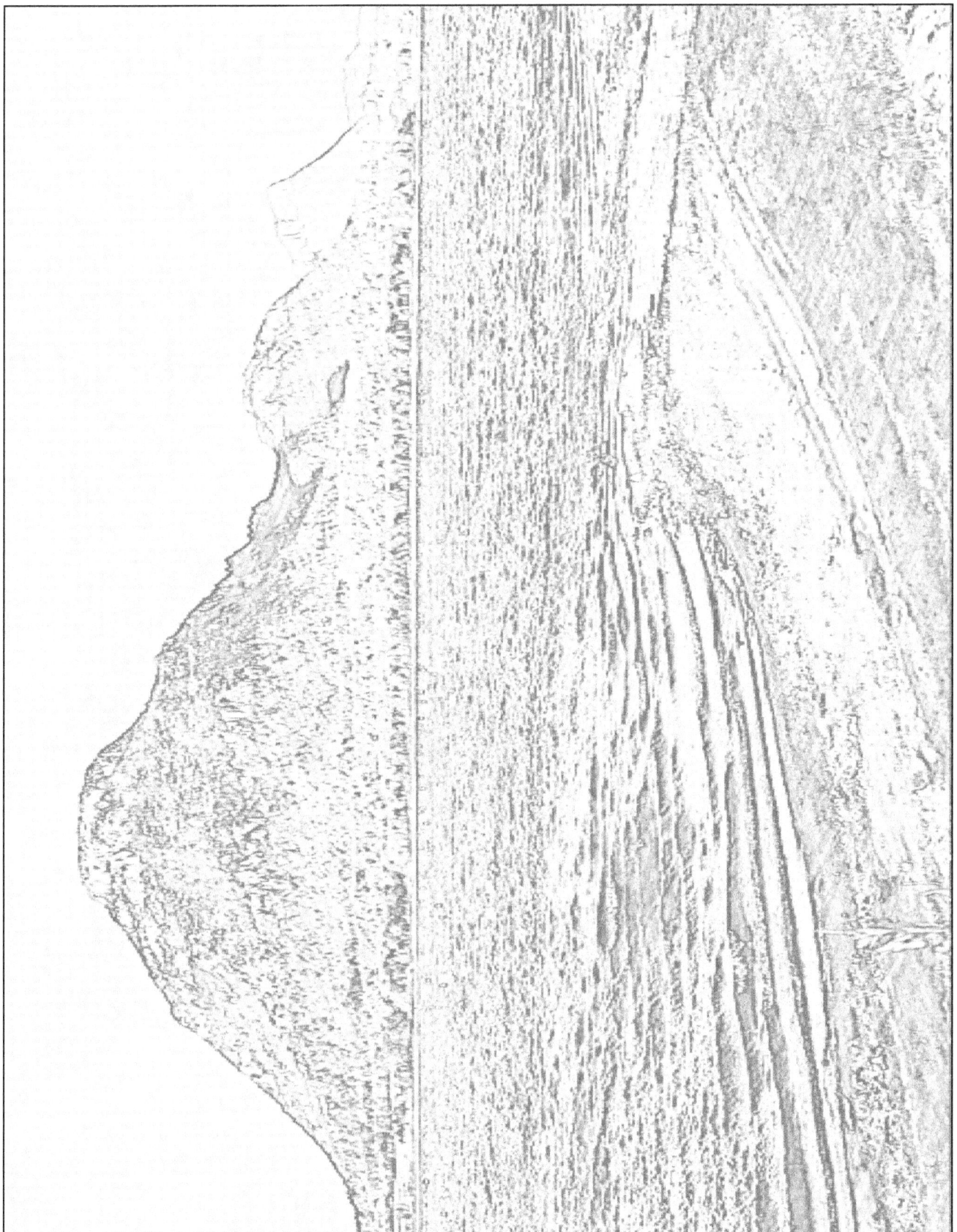

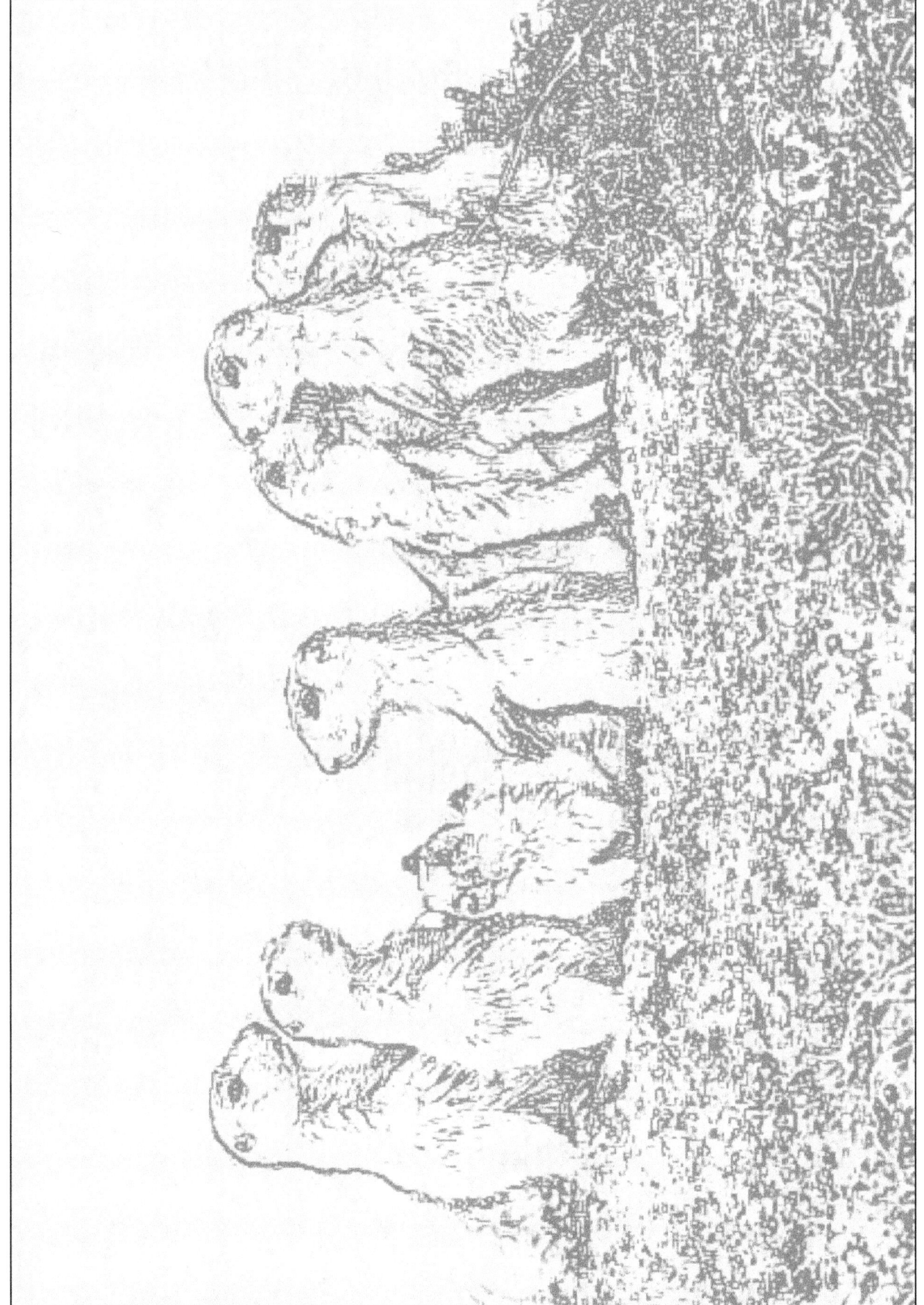

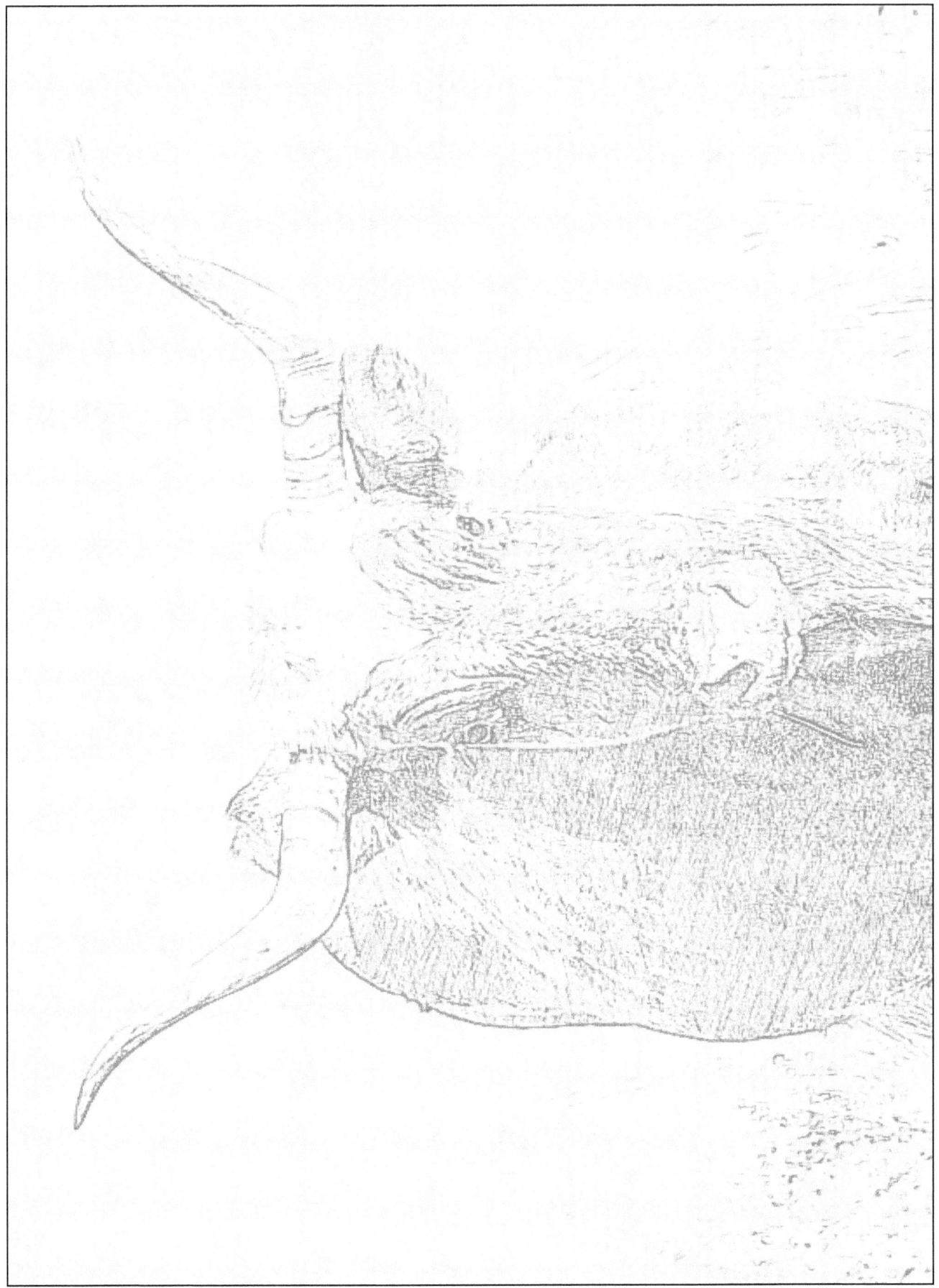

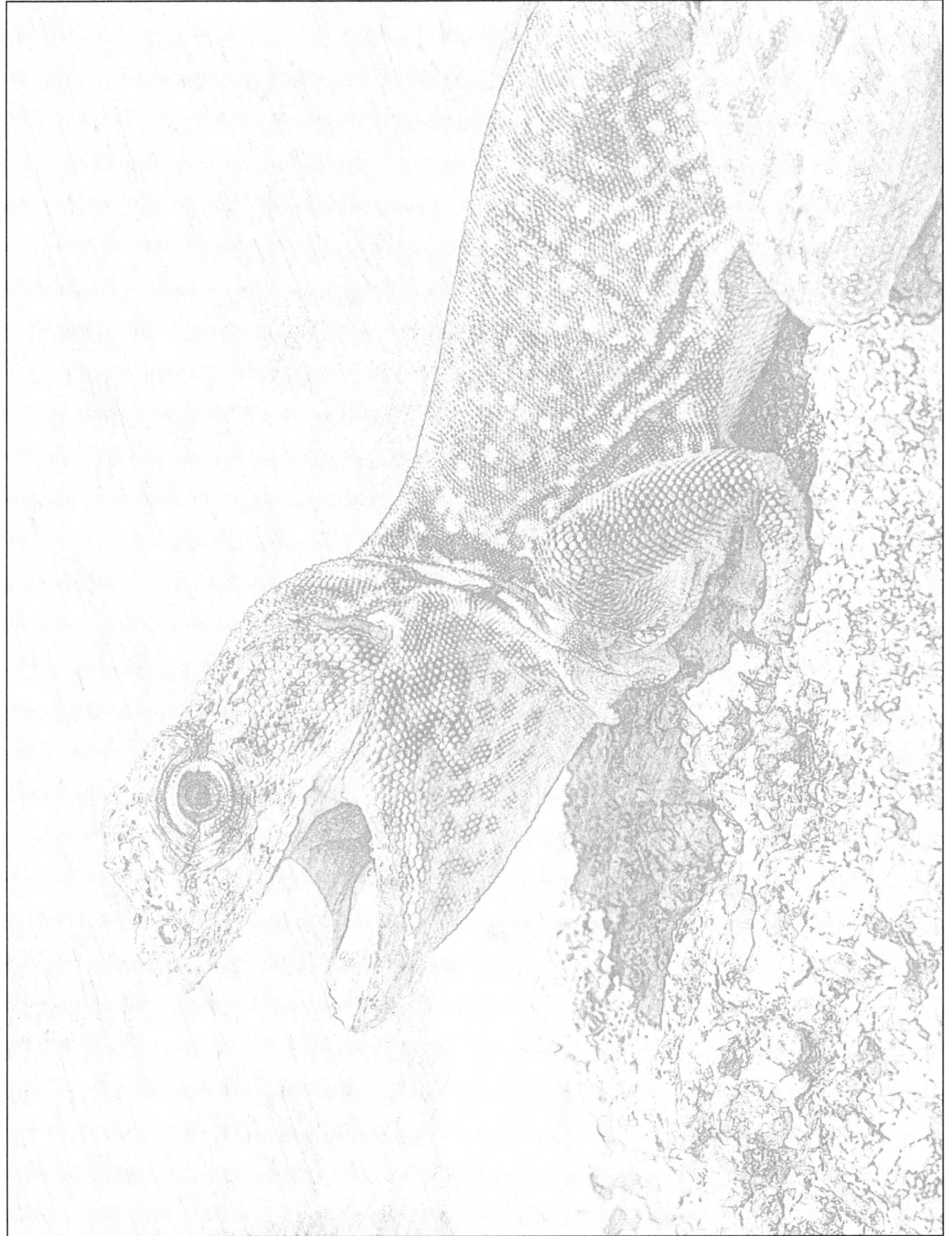

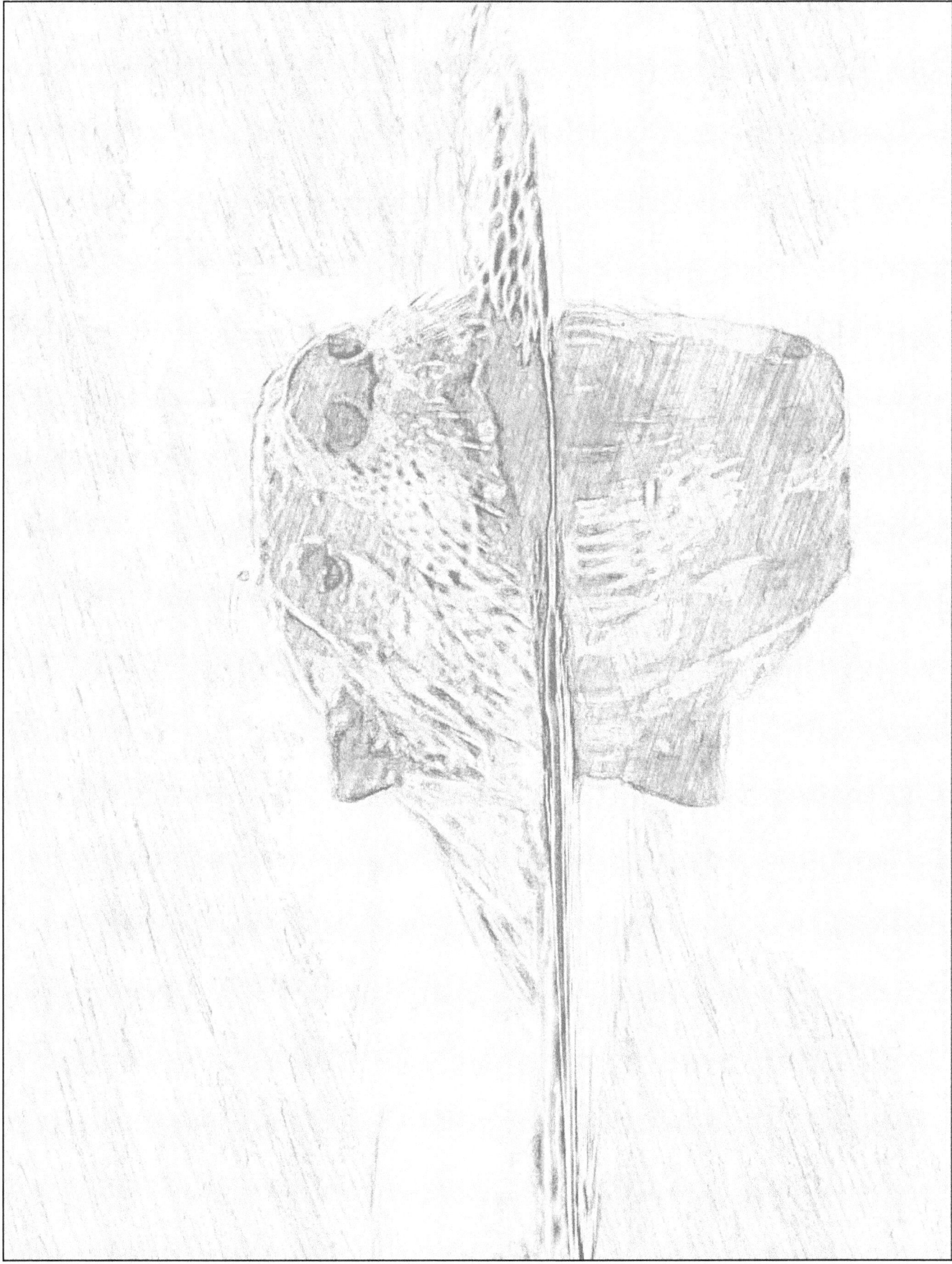

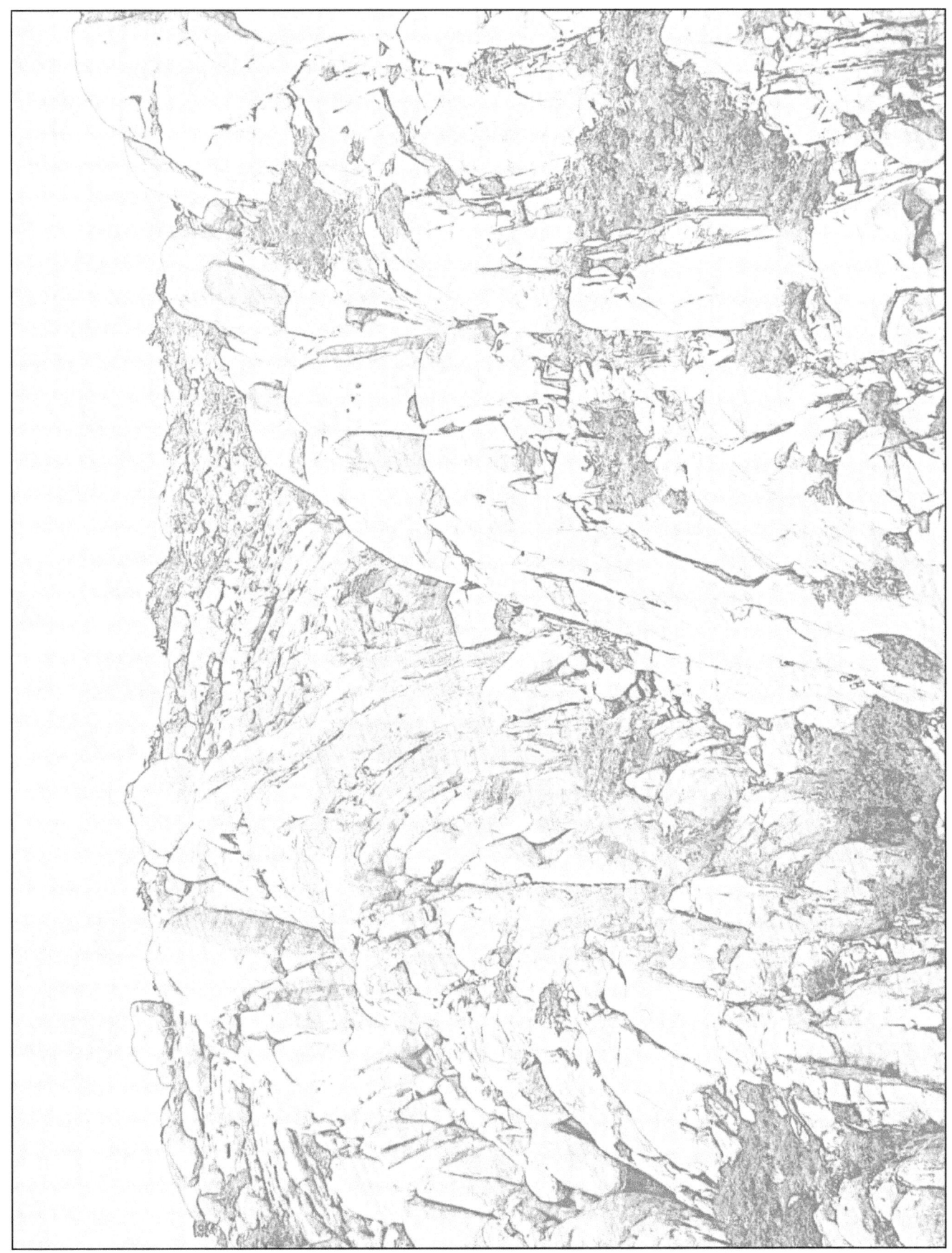

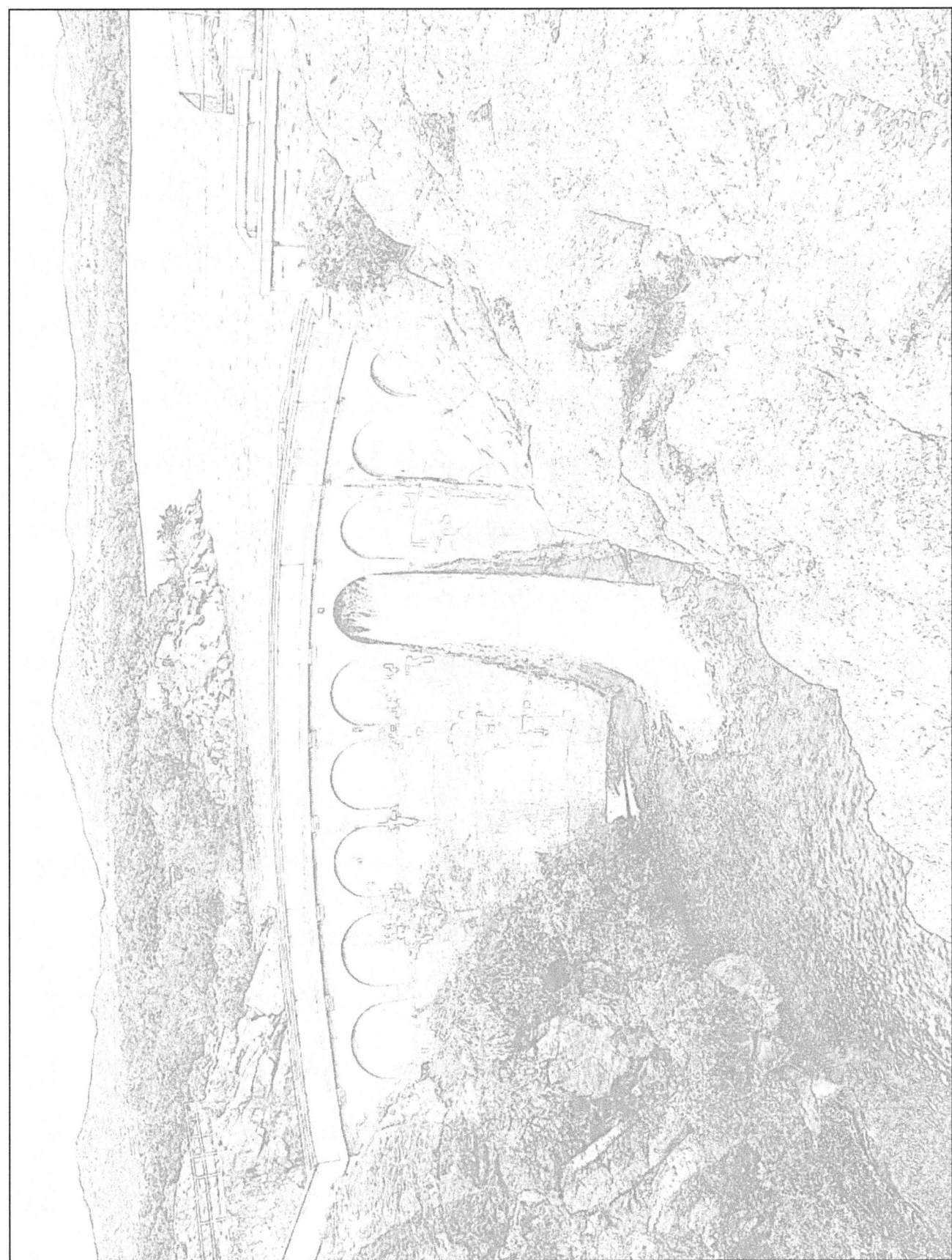

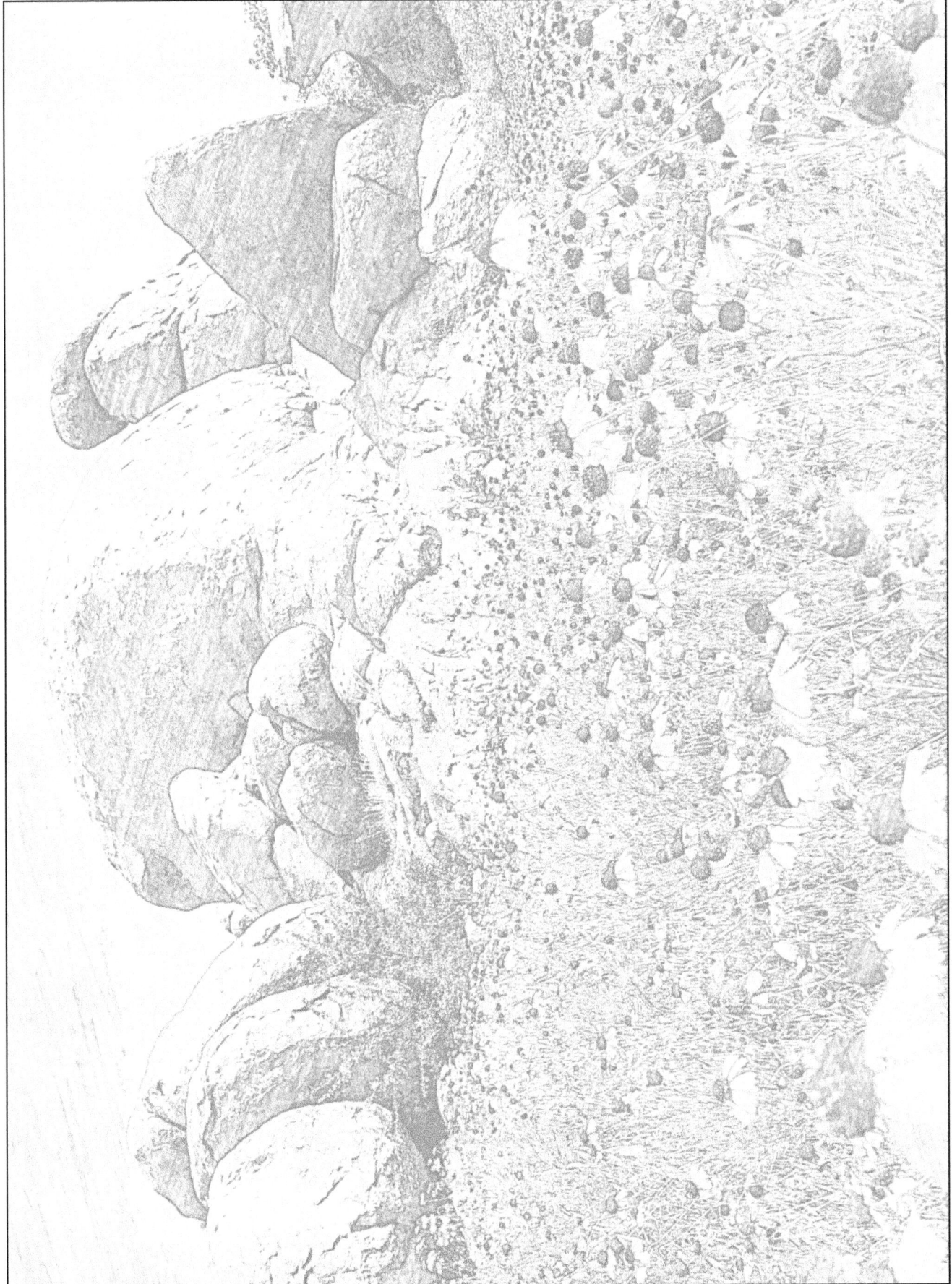

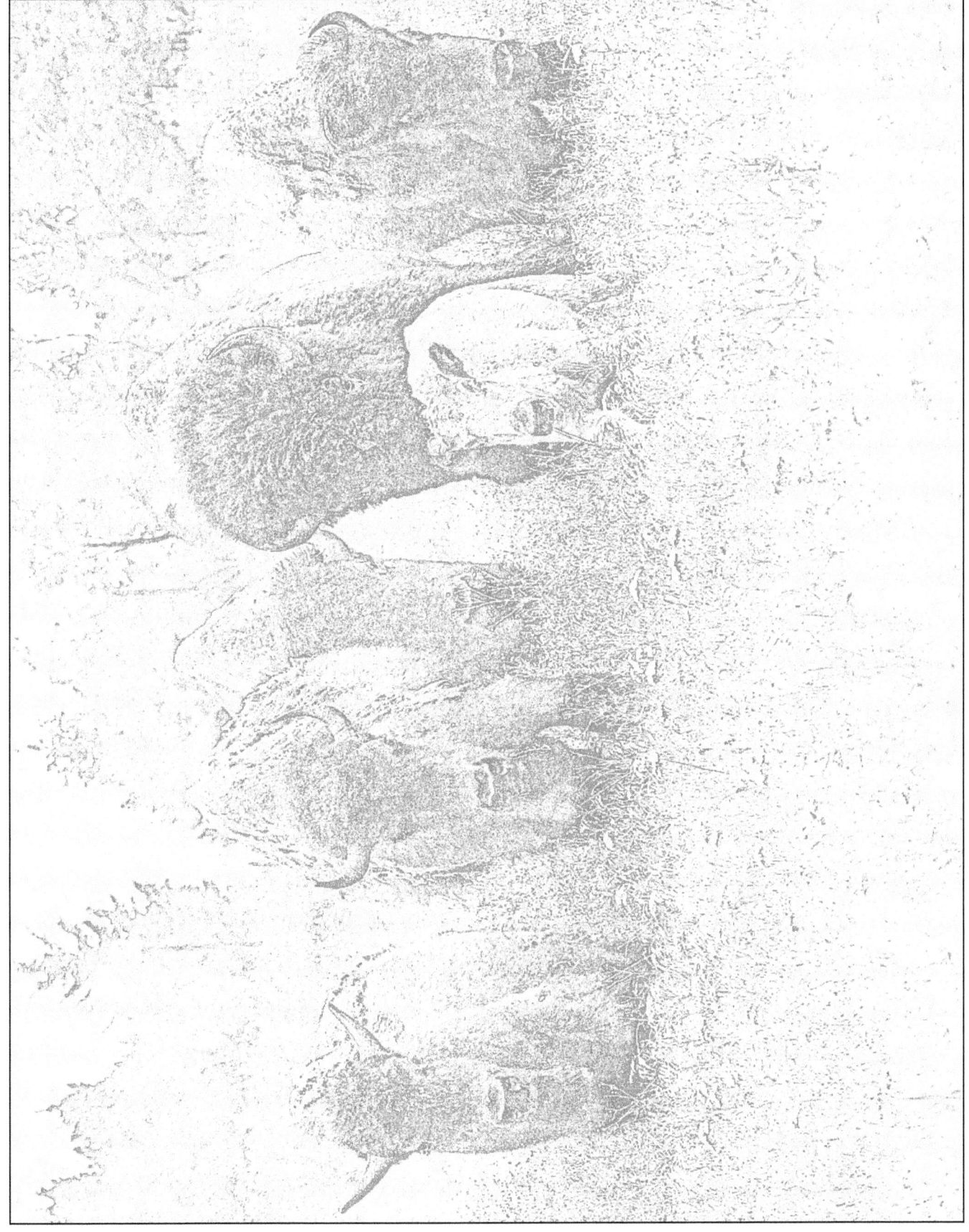

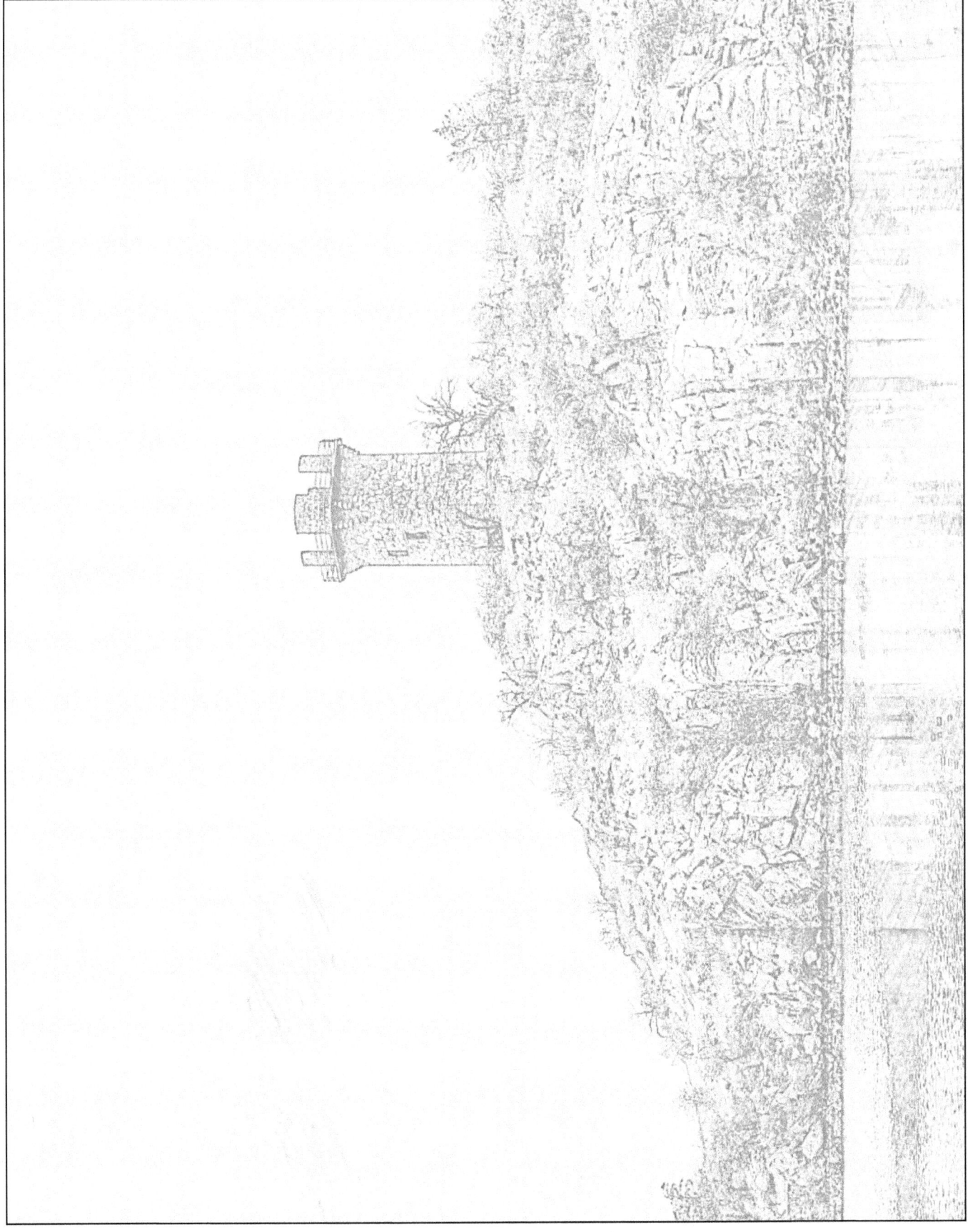

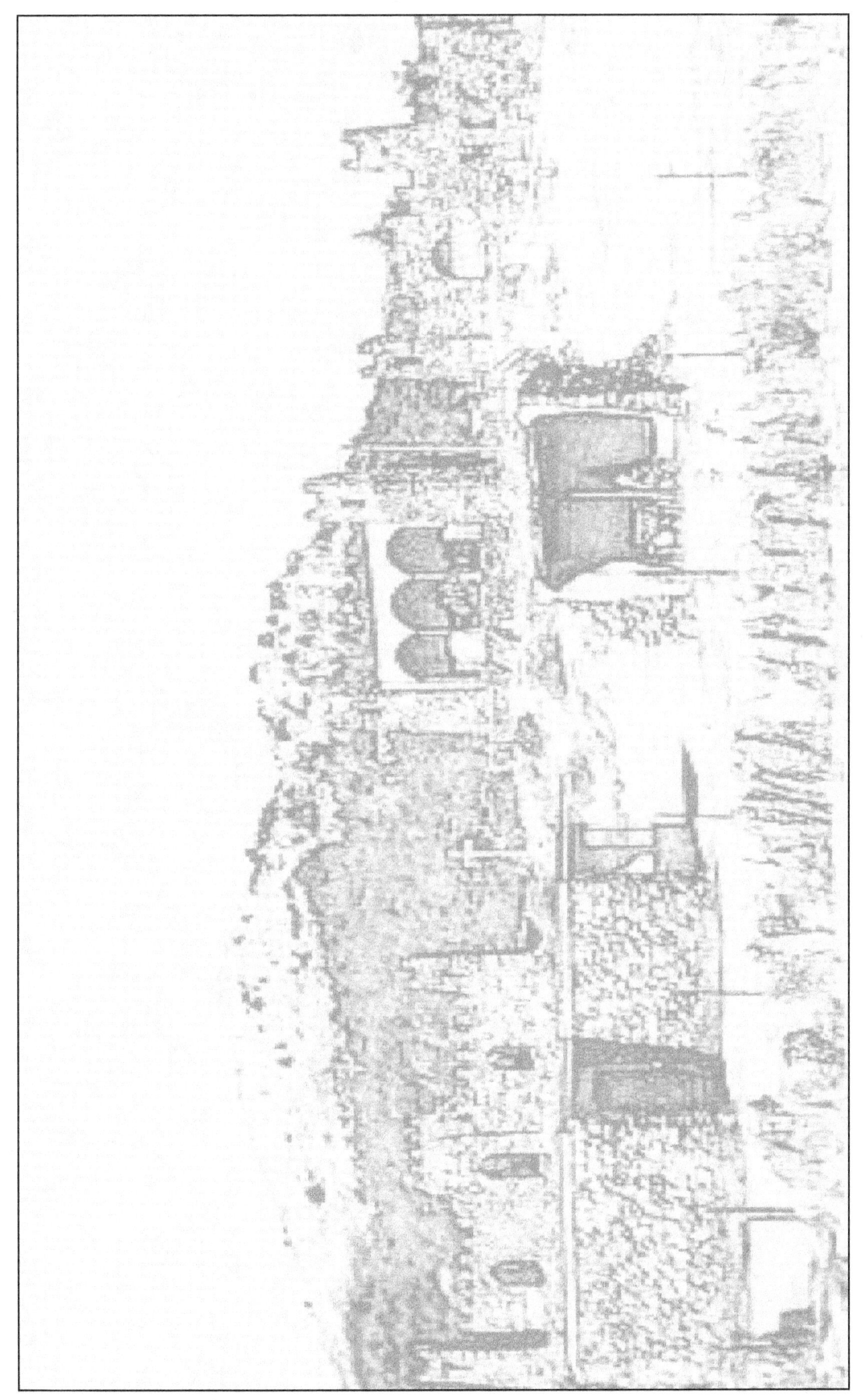

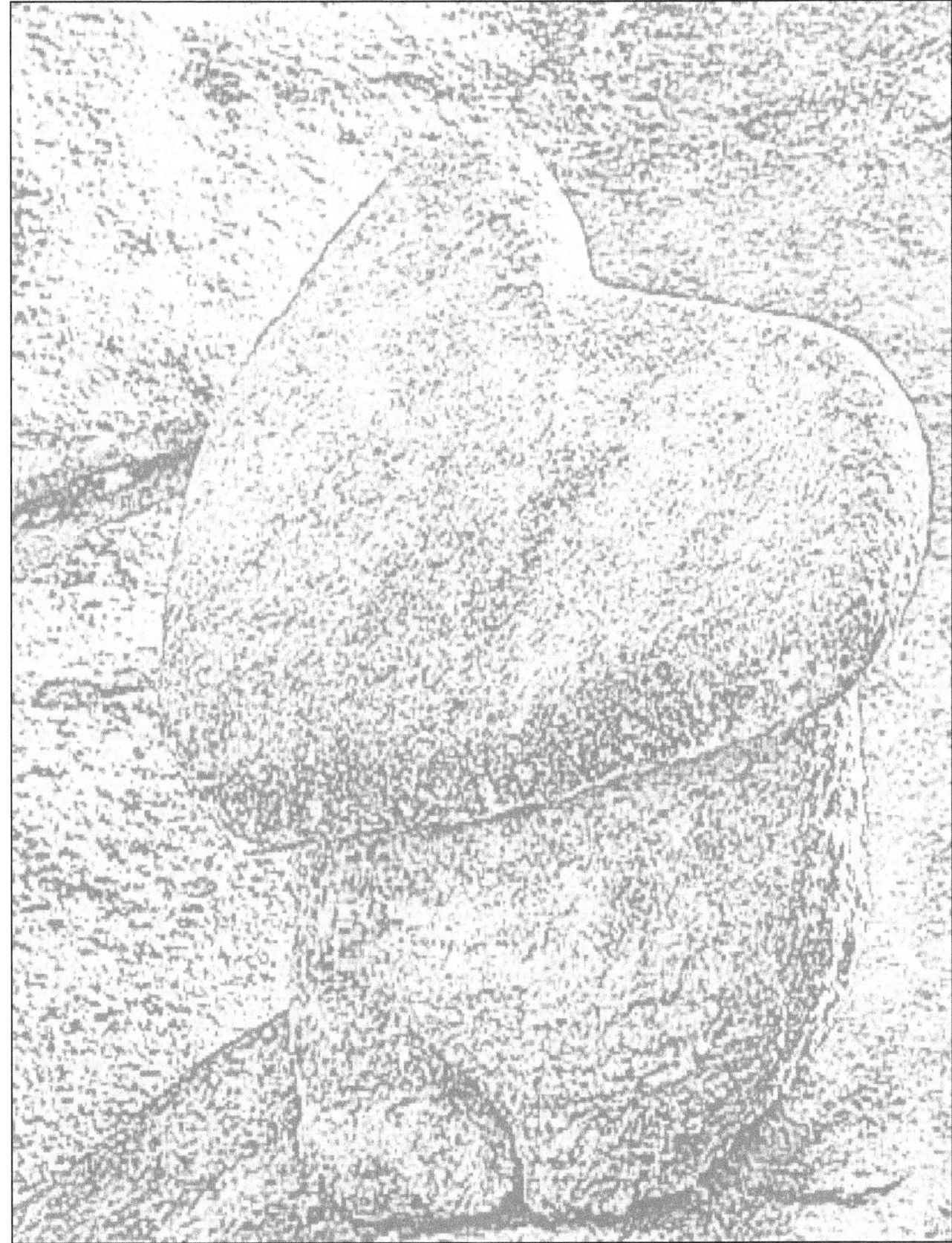

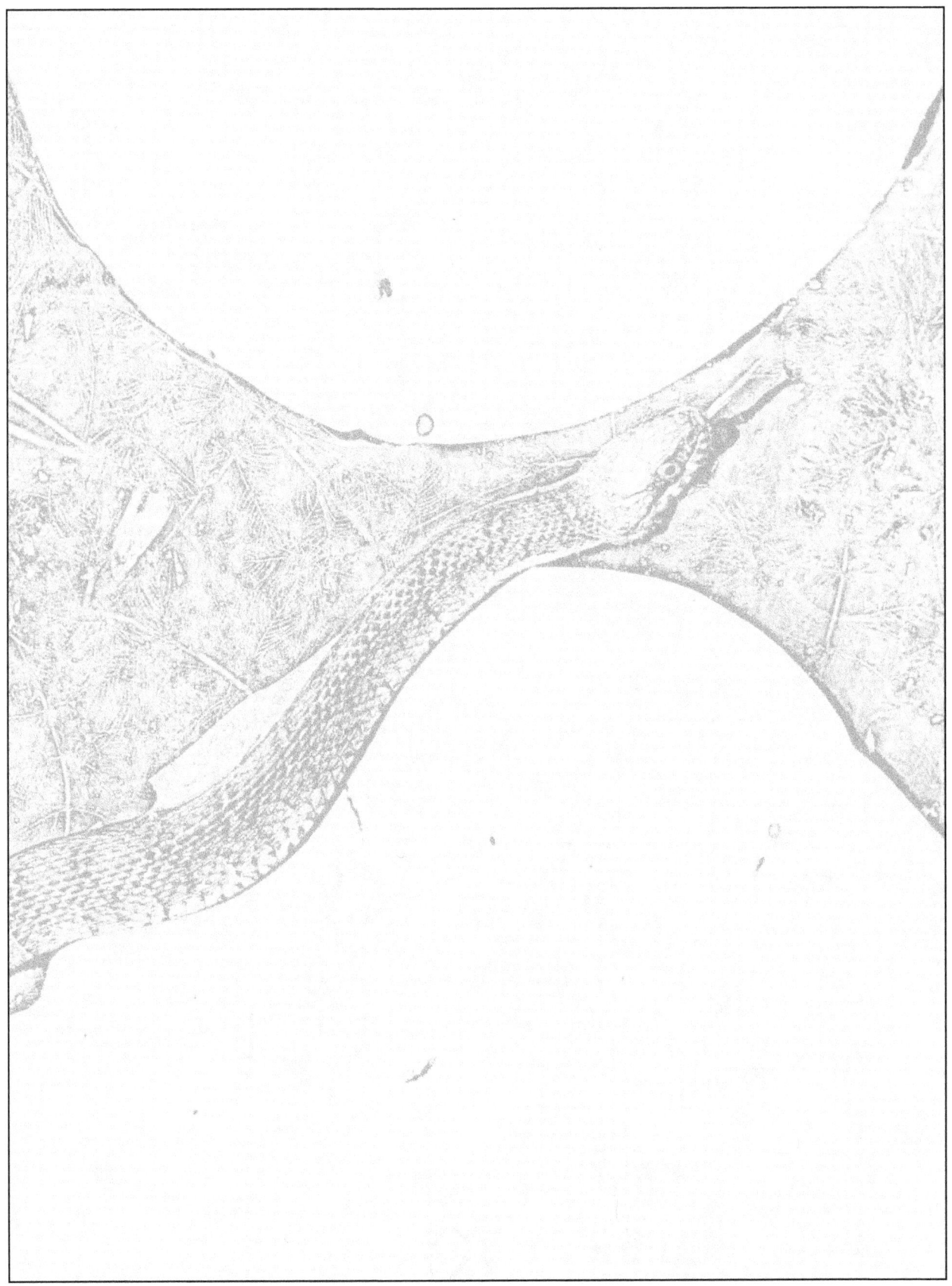

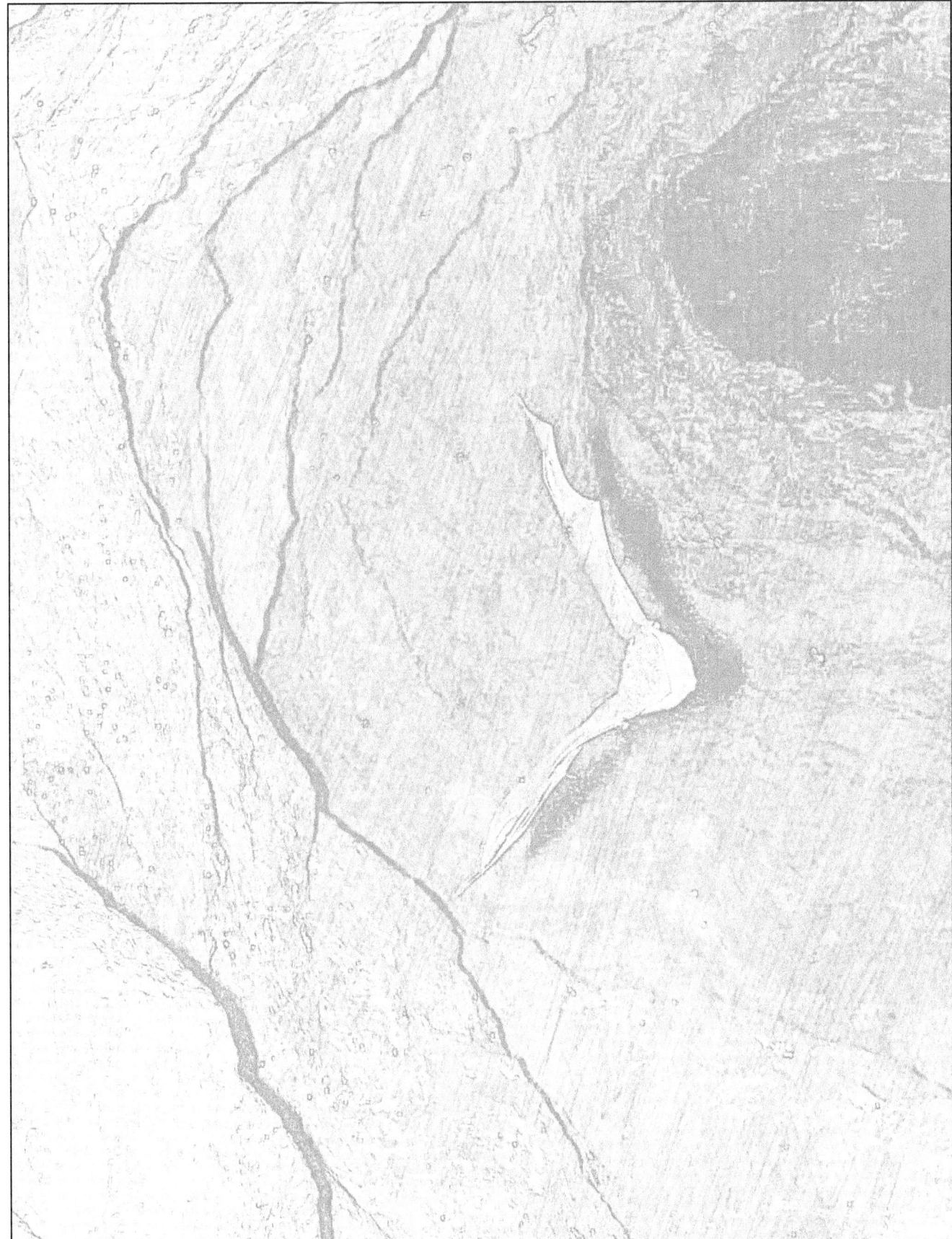

Visitor Center

The Refuge Visitor Center is located at the junction of State Highways 115 and 49. Dioramas and hands-on exhibits complement fine art, sculptures, and exquisite taxidermy. The four major habitat types, rock lands, aquatic, mixed-grass prairie, and cross timbers, are highlighted. A night exhibit reveals the sounds after dark, while a history rail overlooks mountain scenery from picture windows. The auditorium presents programs throughout the day. There is no fee for visiting the center. Maps, books, pamphlets, and other information on wildlife and wild lands are available in the center's bookstore/ gift shop. The America the Beautiful Pass can be obtained from the Visitor Center.

Visitor Center Hours Open
9:00 a.m. to 5:00 p.m. daily. Closed Thanksgiving, Christmas, and New Year's Day.

For General Information: (580) 429-2197
For Tour Reservations: (580) 429-2151

Directions: From I-44 take Highway 49 (exit 45). Go west 10 miles to the Refuge gate. If coming from Highway 62, take Highway 115 (Cache exit) north to the Refuge Gate. You will find leaflet dispensers inside each of the Refuge gates that have maps and information.

Activities Available

- *Camping*
  Reservations, fees and permits available through the Welcome Center.

- *Trails and Hiking*
  Free of charge, seven days a week from sunrise to sunset. This is where you can enjoy wildlife-related activities, including wildlife watching, hiking, and photography. Sixteen designated trails of varying lengths total over 30 miles of nature trails that offer many exciting opportunities to enjoy and explore this biologically rich refuge.

- *Fishing*
  Fishing, in accordance with state and federal regulations, is permitted in all of the refuge lakes in the public use area

- *Hunting*
  Annual controlled hunts for white-tailed deer and elk are conducted. The application process and random drawings are administrated through the Oklahoma Department of Wildlife Conservation. Applications must be submitted in April. For all regulations, contact the Refuge

- *Boating*

- *Picnicking*
  Boulder, Lost Lake, Sunset, and Mt. Scott provide visitors with a variety of settings for picnicking. Picnic hours are posted at area entrances.

- *Tours and Special Programs*
  Wichita Mountains Wildlife Refuge offers many unique programs and tours, some of which venture into the Special Use Area of the refuge. A current schedule of programs is available at the Visitor Center, on the Refuge website, or by visiting: **www.friendsofthewichitas.org**

Wichita Mountains Wildlife Refuge Facts and Questions

When was it established?
The Refuge was first established in 1901 as a Forest Reserve by President William McKinley just prior to the area being opened to settlement. In 1905, President Theodore Roosevelt re-designated the area as the Wichita Forest and Game Preserve. Congress designated the Wichita Mountains as a National Wildlife Refuge in 1936.

How big is it?
The Wichita Mountains Wildlife Refuge includes 59,020 acres located in Comanche County in Southwestern Oklahoma.

How old are the Mountains
The granite mountains were formed over 500 million years ago.

Wildlife Reintroductions
American bison: In 1907, 15 bison were brought back to the southern plains by railcar from the New York Bronx Zoo. The refuge bison herd is presently maintained at 650 head.

Elk: One bull elk was released on the Refuge in 1908. Twenty more cows and bulls were brought from the Jackson Hole area in 1911 and 1912. About 700 elk range on the Refuge today.

Texas longhorn cattle: In 1927, the Sixty-ninth Congress appropriated funds to purchase 30 longhorns. The herd now numbers about 300 head.

Facility development The CCC (Civilian Conservation Corps) were instrumental in the 1930's in constructing 15 concrete dams for permanent water areas and most of the 8-foot high big game boundary fence.

Visitors The Refuge attracts over 1.5 million visitors each year.